FIVE
SMOOTH
STONES
for
PRAYER
WARRIORS

Insights from the Prayer of Acts 4
on Praying with Depth and Focus

MARK DRINNENBERG

FIVE SMOOTH STONES FOR PRAYER WARRIORS

Insights from the Prayer of Acts 4 on Praying with Depth and Focus

By Mark Drinnenberg

writingsbymark@gmail.com
www.markdrinnenberg.com

ONWORD Publishing LLC, McHenry, Illinois.

ISBN: 978-1-7378888-0-2

Dedication

I dedicate this book to Nancy,
the prayer warrior I married.

TABLE OF CONTENTS

ACKNOWLEDGMENTS

Great thanks go to those who worked with me to make this book what it would not have been without their expertise. Miriam Rogers, who edited my words, making sure they are correct and flow well. Ulrika Towgood, who created the layout that makes the book's pages look their best. Kristen Ingebretson, whom I found through Reedsy.com, designed the first thing people see, the cover. Interacting with them was a delight, and I am thrilled with the work they have done.

Two people provided great encouragement that I should write a book. My wife, Nancy, is my biggest cheerleader and has known all along that I should be a writer. Rosalie Stickling, who was a member of the church I pastored when this effort began, told me numerous times that I should write.

Three pastor friends of mine may not even know why their names would appear in this acknowledgment, but each one had shared with me something that contributed to the outcome of this book. Their names are Doug Stelzig, Jerry Scott, and John Pennell. To you I say, "Thank you. And if you are wondering why, please don't hesitate to ask."

The Red House Writers Collective, which I joined just after finishing the initial draft of this book, provided encouragement, advice, and accountability to stick with it and turn that first draft into a finished product. They continue to provide such things as I engage in further writing projects.

The congregation at what used to be known as the Living Word Fellowship was the first to hear the ideas presented in this book. Though the Lord has taken us all to different locations, I love you and thank you for listening as I taught God's Word. It was a privilege to be your pastor.

Finally, exceeding great gratitude to the Lover of my soul—my Savior and Lord, Jesus Christ, by whose blood we become children of God by faith, and to Whom we are invited to draw near with confidence "to the throne of grace, that we may receive mercy and find grace to help in time of need" (Hebrews 4:16).

INTRODUCTION

THE BATTLE BEFORE US

It must have been exciting for young David as the Israel-ite army came into view. Not old enough to be a soldier, his father, Jesse, had sent him to take some supplies to his older brothers on the front lines and bring back news of the battle. This was quite a moment for a boy who typically spent more time with sheep than with people.

As he drew near to the battle lines, his excite-ment turned to disappointment in the soldiers he likely admired. A Philistine warrior, Goliath by name, battle-hardened and huge, was taunting Israel's troops and had them quaking in their sandals.

Goliath had just put forth a challenge to Israel: "Send out your best warrior to do battle with me, one-on-one. If he defeats me, we will be your servants. But if I defeat him, you will be our servants." No one on the Israelite side had any interest in accepting this challenge. Whenever they saw the man, they all fled from him in great fear.

David had a different response. He could not believe God's army would fear this pagan soldier, and he said as much: "Who is this uncircumcised Philistine that he should defy the armies of the living God?" David would accept the challenge.

David's older brothers saw *their* fear suddenly turn to disgust at the thought of their kid brother showing them up. "Just go back and watch over your few sheep," they said. But David would not be deterred. When word reached King Saul that David was talking about fighting Goliath, Saul sent for him. David said to Saul,

"Let no one lose heart on account of this Philistine; your servant will go and fight him." The king assessed that David was too young to take on this task, but David managed to convince Saul that the Lord would give him victory over this uncircumcised Philistine. (1 Samuel 17)

Conventional wisdom would dictate that if an inexperienced youth were going to fight a man so strong that the head of his spear weighs as much as a modern-day bowling ball, the lad should at least dress for the occasion. And so, Saul put his own armor on David and strapped his own sword to David's side. There was a problem, though. Saul was a grown man who was head and shoulders above any other man in Israel while David was a mere youth. Unable even to walk in Saul's armor, David took it all off to face Goliath in his regular attire with no weapon but a sling. On his way out to meet the oversized Philistine, he stopped by a brook to pick up ammo for his sling—five smooth stones. It was all he would need. In fact, it was *more* than he would need. The battle was the Lord's.

Every Christian is involved in a battle. Ours, though, is not against a physical foe. It is a spiritual battle in which we face forces that would seek to hinder the effectiveness of our service to God and destroy our walk with God. The apostle Paul tells us, "We do not wrestle against flesh and blood, but against the rulers, against the authorities, against the cosmic powers over this present darkness, against the spiritual forces of evil in the heavenly places" (Ephesians 6:12).

We fight the spiritual battle on three major fronts; the same fronts we faced before we knew Christ. Paul mentions them in Ephesians 2:

And you were dead in the trespasses and sins in which you once walked, following the course of this world, following the prince of the power of the air, the spirit that is now at work in the sons of disobedience—among whom we all once lived in the passions of our flesh, carrying out the desires of the body and the mind, and were by nature children of wrath, like the rest of mankind. (Ephesians 2:1-3)

Did you see them in there? The trio of fronts on which we fight the spiritual battle are (1) this world, (2) the prince of the power of the air, and (3) our flesh. You may have heard them slightly rearranged and restated *the world, the flesh,* and *the devil.* Let's examine them.

The World

"The course of this world" has to do with how the world thinks and does things and what it considers to be important. It has to do with how it measures success with a mindset that runs contrary to God's values and purposes.

When the psalmist wrote in Psalm 1:1-2, "Blessed is the man who walks not in the counsel of the wicked, nor stands in the way of sinners, nor sits in the seat of scoffers," he was saying that blessing is not found in doing things the world's way. He went on to write of the blessed person, "his delight is in the law of the LORD, and on his law he meditates day and night." In other words, the way of blessing is not found in the world's ways but in a life that delights in God's Word, being thoroughly governed by it. The blessed man evaluates the world, forms opinions, sets goals, and determines what is important on the basis of what God's Word says. The world fights against God's best for our lives while the Word calls us *to* God's best.

11

We can see just how contrary the ways of the world are to the ways of God when we look at Jesus' introduction to the Sermon on the Mount, also known as the Beatitudes (Matthew 5:3-12).

- *Blessed are the poor in spirit, for theirs is the kingdom of heaven.*
- *Blessed are those who mourn, for they shall be comforted.*
- *Blessed are the meek, for they shall inherit the earth.*
- *Blessed are those who hunger and thirst for righteousness, for they shall be satisfied.*
- *Blessed are the merciful, for they shall receive mercy.*
- *Blessed are the pure in heart, for they shall see God.*
- *Blessed are the peacemakers, for they shall be called sons of God.*
- *Blessed are those who are persecuted for righteousness' sake, for theirs is the kingdom of heaven.*
- *Blessed are you when others revile you and persecute you and utter all kinds of evil against you falsely on my account. Rejoice and be glad, for your reward is great in heaven, for so they persecuted the prophets who were before you.*

When Jesus spoke these words, he turned the world's thinking on its head. Probably the only item on this list that the world would give a hearty *amen* to is "Blessed are the peacemakers." However, most of the people that Jesus says are blessed would likely be considered by the world to be weak and defeated and in undesirable situations. The world cannot conceive of things like being poor in spirit or mournful as blessings. To many in the world, meekness is weakness. And why should one be merciful when revenge can be so sweet? Food and drink are wonderful things, the world would say, but what's this business about hungering and thirsting for righteousness when sin is so much fun? And a pure heart? What do you think this is, the Victorian age? And don't even get me started on the idea that being persecuted could in any way, shape, or form be considered a blessing! they might add.

No wonder the psalmist says in Psalm 1 that we should not take our cues from the world. The world's values and pursuits run directly counter to the places where Jesus said blessing is to be found. And we are bombarded by the values of the world at every turn. They're in the music we listen to, the TV shows we watch, the movies we attend, our conversations in the break room at work, our educational system, and just about everywhere else. Winning the battle on this front takes active, regular study of the Bible and conscious evaluation of the things we see and hear. Passivity in this area will almost certainly lead to spiritual defeat.

The Flesh

When we speak of *flesh* in this sense, we are not talking about the literal skin on our bodies but rather, what Paul refers to in the Ephesians passage above as "the passions of our flesh." This is the *if-it-feels-good, do-it* approach to life; the *it's-all-about-me* way of looking at things. Paul gives us a list of what he calls "the works of the flesh" in Galatians 5:

> *Now the works of the flesh are evident: sexual immorality, impurity, sensuality, idolatry, sorcery, enmity, strife,*

jealousy, fits of anger, rivalries, dissensions, divisions,
envy, drunkenness, orgies, and things like these. (Gala-
tians 5:19b-21a)

How contrary to the life of the One who took on flesh
and bore our sins in His body upon a tree! (cf. Colossians
1:22; 1 Peter 2:24)

The flesh draws us away from communion with
God in that when we set our minds on the things of the
flesh, they are not set on the things of the Spirit (Romans
8:5). The flesh draws us away from fellowship with others in that it promotes jealousy and strife in our hearts
(1 Corinthians 3:3).

The flesh is such a tricky foe because catering to
its desires is so natural for us. It can take great disci-
pline—planning, even—to avoid fleshly temptations
like illicit sex, overindulgence in alcohol, self-righteous
outbursts, and other things that may make us feel good,
if even for a moment. The flesh is self-serving. It regularly desires things that promise us pleasure but are, in
fact, unrighteous and oftentimes destructive. No wonder
the Bible instructs us to deny our flesh (Matthew 16:24;
Romans 8:13).

Those who have no regard for God or His Word
do not typically think in terms of denying their flesh.
To them, satisfying their fleshly desires is like scratching
an itch. "If I feel like having sex, why shouldn't I go
get that? If life is stressful, why shouldn't I get drunk
or high so I can relax? In fact, even if life is not stressful, why shouldn't I get drunk or high just because I
want to?" It is hard to see the value of denying the
flesh if one does not view life in terms of righteousness
and unrighteousness and does not consider the will of

God in his/her actions and decisions. But the wisdom of the Bible is seen in that when one caters regularly to the flesh's desires, those desires eventually become demands. Things move from "I want this" to "I need this." Following the Bible's teachings and denying the flesh prevents such enslavement.

The Devil

From the time the serpent tempted Eve in the garden, appealing to her pride and inspiring discontentment with the ways of God and promising that her sin would make her be like God, the devil has worked to rob God of His glory in the lives of humans. Satan is a thief who comes only to steal, kill, and destroy (John 10:10). He is subtle, able even to disguise himself as an angel of light (2 Corinthians 11:14). He fires flaming darts that believers must repel with the shield of faith (Ephesians 6:16). Experience shows that those darts come in the forms of things like doubt, despair, hopelessness, lust, discontentment, impatience, jealousy, envy, false assumptions, and so much more. Scriptural descriptions of the devil include *destroyer* (Revelation 9:11), *accuser* (Revelation 12:10), *adversary* (1 Peter 5:8), *dragon and serpent* (Revelation 12:9), *father of lies* (John 8:44), and *tempter* (Matthew 4:3). Among his names are Satan, Lucifer, and Beelzebub. There is nothing good about him, despite the image some have of him as a grinning red figure with a goatee and a pitchfork, a fun-loving character to be portrayed by children and adults on Halloween. He no doubt loves such a false understanding, for it leaves people with the impression that he is no more to be feared than Casper, the friendly ghost. However, it was not concerning a fun-loving, cartoonish being that Peter urged believers to be sober-minded and watchful of, warning us that our "adversary the devil prowls around like a roaring lion, seeking someone to devour" and instructing us to "resist him, firm in your faith" (1 Peter 5:8-9). Satan is a serious and dangerous foe.

In our own strength, we lack the ability to withstand the onslaught of opposition that is constantly launched against us from the world, the flesh, and the devil. Where, then, do we go for help in withstanding such an onslaught? We must go on our knees in our prayer closets and anyplace else we may be found praying.

A Powerful Example of Prayer

In the fourth chapter of the book of Acts, we find the early believers in Jesus faced with an intimidating situation that could have relegated the church of Jesus Christ to obscurity and early death, had the believers tried to handle the intimidation in their own strength. Peter and John had been arrested for preaching Christ in the section of the temple known as Solomon's Portico. The authorities had warned them to stop preaching in the name of Jesus and had threatened them before letting them go. Upon their release, Peter and John went to their fellow believers and related the threats leveled against them by the chief priests and the elders. This was a turning point moment for the early church; threats from such authoritative men were not to be taken lightly. Jesus had charged His followers with being His witnesses to the ends of the earth, but it was clear that doing so could be quite dangerous. Suddenly, the spiritual battle was raging against these believers on all three fronts. The *world* was intimidating them with threats; their *flesh* may have faced the temptation to take the painless route of staying quiet about Jesus; and certainly, *the devil* would have been turning up the heat on their fear. What did they do? They prayed.

This book is about that prayer in Acts 4:24-30. This is not a book about prayer in general but about one specific prayer offered in a moment of great intimidation where a faithless response would have silenced the witness of the church. That early church's effectiveness for Christ—and the spread of the gospel—would have been neutralized if they had listened to the devil's whispers of fear and responded to the world's threats in the weakness of their own flesh.

This prayer has lessons to teach us about remaining steadfast in our faith through the pressures exerted upon us by the world, the flesh, and the devil. It provides a plan for praying when the heat is on and we do not know what to pray. And it provides a grid to help keep us focused when our minds might tend to wander as we pray.

We find in this prayer five principles for seeking God in the midst of the battle. Just as David carried five smooth stones into his battle against the mighty Philistine warrior, so must we bear *five smooth stones*, as it were, as we engage in our spiritual weapon of prayer.

And when they heard it, they lifted their voices together to God and said, "Sovereign Lord, who made the heaven and the earth and the sea and everything in them, who through the mouth of our father David, your servant, said by the Holy Spirit,

"'Why did the Gentiles rage, and the peoples plot in vain? The kings of the earth set themselves, and the rulers were gathered together, against the Lord and against his Anointed'—

for truly in this city there were gathered together against your holy servant Jesus, whom you anointed, both Herod and Pontius Pilate, along with the Gentiles and the peoples of Israel, to do whatever your hand and your plan had predestined to take place. And now, Lord, look upon their threats and grant to your servants to continue to speak your word with all boldness, while you stretch out your hand to heal, and signs and wonders are performed through the name of your holy servant Jesus."

And when they had prayed, the place in which they were gathered together was shaken, and they were all filled with the Holy Spirit and continued to speak the word of God with boldness.

(Acts 4:24-31, ESV)

CHAPTER 1

PRAYING IN LIGHT OF WHO GOD IS

"My dad can beat up your dad!"

Did you ever say that when you were a child? I am pretty sure I did. When we are very young, we may think our dads can do anything. I have memories of my dad proving that to me; or at least at the time, that is how I took it.

I was five years old when Dad challenged me to a footrace in our backyard. We were to run the length of our next-door neighbor's fence and back. On the first leg of the race, Dad stayed right with me. As we turned around to head for the finish line, he ran backward, staying just ahead of me as I laughed hysterically. He won, of course, because Dad could do anything—even win a footrace running backward.

Around that same time, he did something else that in my impressionable mind convinced me of his absolute greatness. We were standing in the front yard, with Dad holding a bucket and a penny. He threw the penny over the house and said, "Come on!" We ran around the house to the backyard where Dad looked to the sky and said, "There it is!" I looked hard for that penny in the sky but did not see it. "Here it comes," Dad said, as he reached over his side to catch the coin. The sound of the penny falling into the bucket amazed me. Dad was so cool! He could do anything!

A childhood notion that a parent can do anything does not typically survive our passage from youth, as I have learned firsthand, both as a son and as a father. Years later, I was thinking back on the coin-in-the-bucket experience when it suddenly dawned on me how Dad would have done it. He must have feigned throwing the penny from the front yard. Then as we ran around the house to the backyard, holding the penny between his thumb and the inside of the bucket, he must have let the penny fall into the bucket at just the right time. I had to laugh when I realized what a simple trick it was! But in my early years of life, Dad caught that penny, proving he could do anything!

We have a heavenly Father who truly *can* do anything; One whose power never fades away or diminishes even a little bit. As we fight the spiritual battles we face as Christians, it is this heavenly Father to whom we pray. We fight our battles on our knees.

As we study the way the early Christians addressed God in this prayer, we will examine how it reveals the first of the "five smooth stones" we must carry into battle.

Sovereign Lord, who made the heaven and the earth and the sea and everything in them. (Acts 4:24b)

This is the first smooth stone for the prayer warrior. Who is this God to Whom we pray? This matters very much, for the power of prayer is not in the act of praying but in the One to Whom we pray. Scripture tells us many things about Him, but our text focuses on two specific truths about God that the original local church leaned hard upon as they cried out to Him in a time of great need. These two truths are He is sovereign and He created everything.

God Is Sovereign

There is one Greek word behind the ESV's "sovereign Lord." It is the word *despotēs*, and we get our English word "despot" from it. Now, when we hear that word in English, we tend to think of cruel, oppressive rulers. Or we might picture a tyrannical ruler with absolute power. However, the word, even in English, does not have to suggest tyranny, but "a ruler with absolute power and authority" (Merriam Webster dictionary). Clearly, the cry of these early Christians was *not* one of calling upon a tyrant. No, they were calling on One whom they could count on to help them in their desperate need, and they used a word that underscored His absolute power and authority.[1] That is what we mean when we say He is sovereign. Whatever He wills goes, and that is a coin that has two sides. Side one says, "God has full power to make a situation turn out the way I would like it to turn out." Side two says, "Not my will, but Thine be done." He is sovereign in that He is able, and He is sovereign in that His will is right, whether we understand it or not—whether we even *like* it or not. His sovereignty means that He is our Master, and we are His servants. We submit to Him, not the other way around. And that goes for our attitude in prayer as well as in everything else.

These early first-century Christians demonstrated that they understood these realities. Addressing God as *despotēs* showed an attitude of submission to the will of the Master of all things. As a Christian, you are not your own but you were bought with a price (1 Corinthians 6:19-20; 7:23). That price was the blood of His Son. These early servants of the living God had no thought of Him as some Santa Claus-type fulfiller of desires. He was not their genie, ready to grant their wishes. They came with no list of demands. Rather, they came in desperation to their sovereign Lord, ready to yield and submit to His perfect will and wisdom.

When we modern Christians come together to pray, is this how it sounds? How about when you go before the Lord by yourself? Do you pray this way? Personally, I have sometimes sounded like an arrogant brat in my prayers to the Lord. I have gone so far as to accuse God. I can even remember saying to Him, "Are you having *fun* with my *life*?" But without fail, He has lovingly humbled me during those times, impressing upon my heart Who He is and who I am. Such times have left me contrite and apologetic before God while still He fills me with a sense of His love.

That God is sovereign also means He is capable of doing whatever He wants to do. Nothing stops or even hinders Him. The prophet Isaiah quotes God on this:

> *For I am God, and there is no other; I am God, and there is none like me, declaring the end from the beginning and from ancient times things not yet done, saying, 'My counsel shall stand, and I will accomplish all my purpose,' calling a bird of prey from the east, the man of my counsel from a far country. I have spoken, and I will bring it to pass; I have purposed, and I will do it. (Isaiah 46:9-11)*

No wonder the apostle John says, "This is the *confidence* that we have toward him, that if we ask *anything* according to his will, he hears us. And if we know that he hears us in whatever we ask, we know that we have the requests that we have asked of him" (1 John 5:14-15, italics added). Notice how John's words speak both of God's sovereign ability and authority. God's sovereign *ability* means that

He is *able* to grant whatever we ask. His sovereign *authority* means that He grants whatever we ask *according to His will*. This smooth stone involves praying with full confidence in God's ability and full submission to His authority. Of course, we do not always know God's specific will, but if we know His Word, which gives us not only specific details on some aspects of His will but also a sense of what His heart might be on a given matter, then we can pray for the kinds of things He wants. When that happens, we will be praying for correct things. If our prayer seems to be in accordance with His will but does not seem to be answered as we would like, then we must bow to His sovereignty and trust His wisdom and love. After all, He whose ability knows no limits is very wise and is also love (1 John 4:8).

God Created Everything

The proof that God can do anything is evident in that He created absolutely everything. That's what that phrase "heaven, the earth, the sea and everything in them" means. There is nothing created that God did not make. He did not make Himself, of course, for He has always been. He seemed to be saying that when Moses asked to know His name and God answered "Yahweh," which means "I am" (Exodus 3:13-14). God's very name carries the idea of existence. He is the only Being whose existence is absolutely necessary. Everything else is only here because He wants it to be here, and that includes you and me! Every created thing—from the largest item in the farthest reaches of space to the smallest molecule on earth—is dependent upon God for its very existence. Apart from Him, nothing would exist, and everything that does exist was created by Him out of nothing. That's what you call power!

Understand that when you come to God in prayer, beset with some problem that seems insurmountable, you come to the One who created everything from nothing. And "everything" includes the elements that make up your seemingly insurmountable problem. There is nothing too big for Him to handle!

While God's creative ability clearly shows Him to be powerful enough to answer our prayers, it also suggests that His mind is wonderfully vast. Just think of the variety and complexity that exists in creation, and understand that God envisioned it all, down to the most microscopic details, before there was even the matter that would make up any of it. In addition to the variety and complexity of creation, think of the immensity of it all. Take, for example, one planet in our solar system—the largest planet, Jupiter. Its volume could hold about 1,300 earths.[2] So if Jupiter is quite huge, and it is only one of multiplied billions of objects in space, how vast must space be? Yet Jupiter, as large as it is, is dwarfed by our sun,[3] and our sun, as large as *it* is, is just an average-sized star.[4] Of the billions and billions of stars in the universe, there are stars that are 100 times larger than our sun,[5] which is huge compared to Jupiter, which is huge compared to the earth. Can you begin to get an idea of the power and creativity of this God who created everything—this God to whom we pray?

Have you ever seen a group of people take on the task of removing a tree stump? It can take hours and hours of hard work just to get one stump out of a four-foot-square piece of ground. But God did not even break a sweat bringing the entire universe into existence by His Word. He said, "Let there be light," and there was light where for all eternity past there had been only darkness. What need can we possibly have that God cannot fill? And along with His ability to do *any*thing, His perfect wisdom ensures that He will always do the *right* thing.

In Romans 11:33-36, Paul gives a good summary of the confidence we can have in praying to our sovereign God.

> *Oh, the depth of the riches and wisdom and knowledge of God! How unsearchable are his judgments and how inscrutable his ways! "For who has known the mind of the Lord, or who has been his counselor? Or who has given a gift to him that he might be repaid?" For from him and through him and to him are all things. To him be glory forever. Amen.*

He mentions "the depth of God's riches," which ensures us that God never lacks what He needs to help us. In addition to this, "the depth of the wisdom and knowledge of God," whose "judgments are unsearchable and whose ways are inscrutable," ensures us that God always knows what He is doing, even when we are confused about it. "Who has known the mind of the Lord," Paul asks, "or who has been His counselor?" The implied answer to each question is no one. We are never in a position to second-guess God, nor does He owe us anything. How often do we approach God in a difficult time with an attitude that suggests we have earned better than what He is delivering or allowing? Paul shoots down that attitude when he asks, "Who has given a gift to [God] that he might be repaid?" Once again, the implied answer is no one. After all, what could we possibly offer to the Creator of everything that would give us any kind of leverage at all with Him? Paul says in verse 36 that these things are true because "from him and through him and to him are all things." In other words, because God is the source, the agent, and the purpose of all things, He is absolutely sovereign over all things and has wisdom that is beyond judgment or question. This is the God to Whom we pray.

God's Greatest Display of Power

As great as it is that the One to Whom we pray is the Creator and Sustainer of absolutely everything, there is something even greater that God does on a regular basis: He turns the lost into the found, rebels into the reconciled, children of darkness into children of light. Our salvation is a *sovereign* work of God; He does it not out of any obligation to us or because we deserve it in any way, but because He *wants* to do it. Redemption is His plan worked out in His way by His power.

We enter into salvation on His terms: by faith in His Son who paid our sin debt on the cross and won our victory through the resurrection. We were chosen in Christ before the foundation of the world (Ephesians 1:4), and Christ died for us while we were yet sinners (Romans 5:8). Clearly, our salvation is a sovereign work of God. It is also a *creative* work in that, when we are saved through faith in Jesus, we become new creations—old things having passed away and all things becoming new (2 Corinthians 5:17). God makes new creations out of sinful wretches like us! Hallelujah!

Imagine the power it took to create the universe and everything in it. Then, try to comprehend the power it takes to turn one rebellious, obstinate heart to the Savior to receive God's gift of salvation. But maybe you have never known this new birth that He gives. Maybe you have never been made into a new creation; maybe you have been religious but are not saved. If so, you need to take care of that before you go any further in this matter of prayer. The work for salvation has already been done for you at the cross. Jesus, in paying the penalty for sin (death), paid your sin debt to God, and He paid it in full, declaring as He drew His last breath, "It is finished." Because of His finished work done on your behalf, the gift of salvation is on the table for you to receive by faith.

Sitting right where you are, you can simply tell God that you want this salvation Jesus has won for you. Believe in Jesus; trust in what He did on the cross for your sake and receive Him as your Savior. There are no hoops to jump through or works to be done to earn it. In fact, salvation cannot be earned, for you could never do enough to pay off the debt of sin that hangs over you. Receive Jesus as your Savior, and you will, in that very instant, become a new creation, possessing eternal life. The Bible says, "To all who did receive him, who believed in his name, he gave the right to become children of God" (John 1:12). If you have not received Him, will you do it now?

Conclusion

All who are in Christ face spiritual battles. They come in the form of temptation to sin; in the form of doubts and fears that plague our hearts through the lies of the devil; in the form of a lost sense of urgency to our faith and to the need to be a witness for Christ. Our battles come from the influences of the world, the lies of the devil, and the desires of the flesh. As we fight on our knees in dependence upon our sovereign, creator God, be sure to have this smooth stone in your arsenal: praying in light of who God is. Doing so will enable you to pray boldly, with faith and assurance, and in accordance with the heart of God.

THOUGHTS & PRAYERS

_____

_____

_____

_____

_____

_____

_____

_____

_____

_____

_____

_____

_____

_____

_____

_____

_____

_____

_____

_____

THOUGHTS & PRAYERS

CHAPTER 2

PRAYING IN LIGHT OF WHAT GOD'S WORD SAYS

Once I was at an informal gathering of Christians who had come together to spend time with a ministry leader someone had brought to the area. As we were talking, this leader mentioned being a big fan of either the University of Alabama or Auburn University (I do not remember which) football. She spoke of being present at one of their meetings on the football field. With great humor and exuberance, she described how it had been a close game and how she, being caught up in the emotion of the moment, had cried out to the Lord to let her team win. Her comments were made in fun, but they led someone in the group to ask a serious question, "How do you think the Lord feels about people praying for football games?" Her answer was witty and disarming, "I think He's just happy we're praying at all."

Have you ever prayed a prayer like that? I know I have. Have you prayed for your favorite sports team to win the big game? Of course, what are we to do with the fact that surely other believers are praying for the opposing team to win? Did you ever pray that somebody who made your heart go pitter-patter would feel the same way about you? But then, maybe someone else was praying the same thing about that person. Have you ever prayed for a light to stay green, but it changed to red just before you got to it? Perhaps someone sitting in the cross-traffic was praying for the opposing light to turn green? Did that person's prayer trump yours or did the light merely run its cycle?

Is there value in praying such prayers? Perhaps that ministry leader was right: God is just happy we're praying at all. Certainly, going through the day praying about the details of the day and the things that are on our hearts does keep us conscious of the Lord's presence in our lives. On the negative side, though, constantly praying for the Lord to intervene in things where He does not seem likely to do so could cause our faith to take a hit, especially as we find those green lights nearly always seeming to turn red. It seems we could use a guide on this matter of prayer.

The Bible—the Word of God—is our guide. It is in the Bible where we learn who this God is. In its pages we learn about our fallen state and how to be restored to relationship with God. It is where we learn what the Lord is *like*, what He *desires*, and what He *expects*. The Bible is our guide for life in general, including our life of prayer.

As we study the Scriptures, we will not really find the hope-and-a-prayer approach to praying that might lie behind prayers for green lights and parking spaces. What we do find is an amazing promise that we will receive the things we pray for when we have prayed for things in accordance with God's will (1 John 5:14-15). So, what sorts of things constitute God's will? The answer to that is also found in the Bible. All of this being the case, when fighting the spiritual battle against the world, the flesh, and the devil, we had better be certain that the Word of God is in our arsenal. We need to pray in light of what God's Word says. That is the second smooth stone for the prayer warrior.

That is what the earliest Christians did in Acts chapter 4 as they cried out to God in the midst of the battle:

"Sovereign Lord...who through the mouth of our father David, your servant, said by the Holy Spirit, 'Why did the Gentiles rage, and the peoples plot in vain? The kings of the earth set themselves, and the rulers were gathered together, against the Lord and against his Anointed'—for truly in this city there were gathered together against your holy servant Jesus, whom you anointed, both Herod and Pontius Pilate, along with the Gentiles and the peoples of Israel." (Acts 4:24-27)

They understood that the responses of the world to Christ, even down to the recent frightening events involving Herod and Pilate, were just as God's Word had said things would be. So confident were these believers in the Word of God that they used it to interpret the hardship in which they now found themselves, and they prayed in light of it. Their prayer was not the prayer of people who had been blindsided by their difficult circumstances. Rather, it poured forth from an awareness that the difficulties surrounding them were part of God's plan, a fact they were able to discern because they knew the Scriptures. And, more than just *knowing* the Scriptures, these saints *submitted* to its authority.

The words they quote "from the mouth of [their] father David" are found in Psalm 2:1-2. These praying saints recognized that what David said ultimately came from a higher source than himself—David had uttered them "by the Holy Spirit." In other words, while Psalm 2 was authored by David, he wrote words that came from God. These are not simply the writings of a great man and king, or mere sayings that people find comforting. They are not just great Jewish poetry, they are the Word of God, for they come from the Spirit of God.

This early Christian prayer meeting took place a few decades before Paul would write in 2 Timothy 3:16, "All Scripture is breathed out by God and is profitable for teaching, for reproof, for correction, and for training in righteousness." Many years after this Acts 4 prayer was prayed, one of those present would write that "no prophecy was ever produced by the will of man, but men spoke from God as they were carried along by the Holy Spirit" (2 Peter 1:21). That is the understanding the church in Acts 4 had about the words uttered by David in Psalm 2.

The confidence these early Christians had in the Scriptures was well-founded. Time and again, the Bible's accuracy suggests that it is more than just another book. While the primary purpose of this present writing is not to defend the divine authorship of Scripture, let us nevertheless consider five facts that lend support to the idea that the Bible is more than a book of mere human authorship.

1. *The Jews remaining an ethnically identifiable race for 1,900 years with no homeland.*

When the Romans sacked Jerusalem and destroyed the temple in AD 70, the Jews scattered to the four winds and were often unwelcome wherever they landed. Of course, there would have been some intermarriage that occurred over 1,900 years, and it would seem that without a place to call home and being scattered to so many places distant from each other, the Jews would have gotten absorbed into the places where they dwelt. Yet, they remained an ethnically identifiable race, a race that saw six million souls slaughtered under the Nazi Third Reich, and a nation that finally returned to its homeland in 1948. Why is this important? Because for the Bible to be true, the covenants God made with Israel demand that the Jews never disappear. The fact that they have remained a race, when so many races that existed all around them in ancient times have disappeared, is strong evidence that the Bible is God-authored.

2. *Closely related to that, the current existence of the nation of Israel.*

One cannot read Bible prophecy without realizing that the nation of Israel must exist in the last days for prophecy to be true. For 1,900 years, there was no geographical nation of Israel. Since 1948, there has been.

3. *Political movements that desire the end-times world described in the Bible.*

There is a growing movement of people who want to abolish national borders. That being the case, the world has never seemed more ready for a one-world government, which is what the Scriptures portray the world would be when the Antichrist rules. There is also a growing movement for religions to homogenize. Consider, for instance, the popular bumper sticker that calls for the world's major religions to "co-exist." This shows a desire of many in the world to have a one-world religion, another end-times prophecy yet to come under the rule of the Antichrist. In addition, a system for implementing the mark of the beast, where everyone must have an identification upon his hand or forehead to be able to buy and sell (Revelation 13:16-18), would be very easy to accomplish with today's technology. The world has never been so ready for the end-times world the Bible describes, a world that could not have been envisioned by even the most creative thinkers when the Bible was being written. Finally, as if on cue, the world is increasingly turning against Israel, which must happen for events to unfold the way the Bible puts them forth.

4. *Archaeological evidence that supports the accuracy of the Bible.*

The Bible has a remarkable record of historical accuracy verified by archaeology. For instance, a 2014 article in *Biblical Archaeology Review* lists fifty Old Testament persons that archaeological evidence demonstrates to have existed. One well-known example is King David. It was long disputed whether he ever existed at all, given that "the personal name David had never appeared in archaeological records, let alone a reference to King David."[6] However, in 1993 a ninth-century BC inscription was found that mentions the victory of a non-Israelite king over 'the king of Israel' and 'the house of David.'"[7] This gave archaeological evidence for the existence of David.

Three years after that article, its author published a follow-up listing three more names.[8] An interesting fact about the fifty-three Bible characters listed in the two articles is that while some are prominent characters in the Bible (e.g., David and Hezekiah), many are not. Some were kings of lesser significance (in terms of their mention in the Bible) who ruled in Israel or Judah, some were kings of other nations, and some were not kings at all. When it is verified that even obscure players in the Bible's story were in fact historical figures, that offers evidence that the biblical writers were not just making up stuff. The world they described is the world that was. Of course, there will always be opportunities for critics to point to people or things in the biblical narrative that have *not* been verified by archaeology and say, "What about *this*?" or "What about *that*?" But such gaps exist in the archaeological records of all ancient histories, biblical or not. Many things from thousands of years ago will never be found. But the Bible's record on such things seems good, which is what one might expect if the Bible is indeed the Word of God. Does this *prove* that the Bible is divinely inspired? No. But it is one more brick in the wall of support for the Bible not to be dismissed as just another book.

5. *The way the Bible's teachings work when practiced in life.*

So many of life's difficulties stem from a failure to live by the Bible's wisdom and teachings. For instance, substance abuse is not an issue for those who heed the Bible's teachings on drunkenness and sobriety. Relational strife often has at its root in things like selfishness and unforgiveness, both of which go against what the Bible says on such matters. The resultant lack of peace felt in the heart of a person who ignores the Bible's admonition on these things can turn to bitterness and begin to spread so that it winds up afflicting more people than the ones involved in the conflict that started it all. Speaking of relational issues, one who follows the Bible's teachings on sex and its proper use will be much less likely to develop a sexually transmitted disease. Of course, if one has an unfaithful spouse who contracts an STD, the innocent spouse will be susceptible to contracting the STD from the one who fooled around, but the whole scenario would happen only because the cheating spouse disobeyed the Bible. And then there is the matter of finances. Risky behavior in that area can often be avoided by applying what the Bible teaches in the handling of one's money.

These few arguments are not going to convince a hardened skeptic. There are, of course, many more arguments that can be (and have been) made. Entire books are written on the subject. I am certainly no expert in these things, but in an age where so many unbelievers seem bent on evangelizing Christians out of their faith, I offer these few bits of evidence, within the flow of this book that is about something else entirely, so that the believer whose faith in God's Word might be faltering can see that there is more to the claims of the Bible's nature as a divinely inspired book than just mere church tradition. The Bible provides wisdom for all of life because it was given to us by the Author of life. It is accurate because it is the Word of God. As such, it makes good sense to use it in our praying. This church in Acts 4 shows us one way to do that. Note how they quoted Psalm 2:1-2 as a *description* of what they were going through while they *prayed* about what they were going through. Knowing Scripture gave them perspective on their situation and helped them to know *how* to pray about that situation.

I love to use Scripture in my prayers because when you pray Scripture *in its proper context* (and that qualifier cannot be emphasized enough), it is comforting and assuring, but also it is convicting and exhorting. Fill your heart with Scripture and your heart will be turned to the Lord. You may be in a situation where you fall to your knees with selfish intent, only to have Scripture, whether open before you or hidden in your heart, humble you and increase your faith. Perhaps some examples would help to explain this. Here are some Scriptures that have often turned up in my prayers over the years, and some ways in which I might pray them.

Examples of Using Scripture in Prayer

In times of confessing sin but not *feeling* forgiven, 1 John 1:9 inevitably comes to mind. It tells me that if I confess my sins, I *am* forgiven. I listen to that verse because it is the Word of God, and I may say something like, "I don't *feel* forgiven right now, Lord. But Your Word tells me I *am* forgiven in Christ. So I thank You for the sacrifice Jesus made on the cross for me, and by faith I claim the forgiveness You have given me. Your Word also tells me that Satan is the accuser of the brethren. I reject his accusations right now and embrace Your forgiveness."

In times of fear, Psalm 23:4 is a goldmine. "Even though I walk through the valley of the shadow of death, I will not fear, for you are with me." Depending on the level of fear you may be facing, you might find yourself repeating that verse over and over, and that is good. But it is also good to move from reciting the verse to talking it through with God in light of what the verse teaches.

For example, "Lord, if even the valley of death, my greatest enemy, is a place where I need not fear, then what could possibly be a situation where I need to set that verse aside and tremble in fear? For it is You who made the heavens and the earth and all that is in them, and it is You who holds them all together. Therefore, is there anything that could take place within the heavens and the earth where You being with me could turn out to be useless? Of course not! You have said You will never leave me nor forsake me, so where is the fearful place or circumstance that could rob me of the safety of Your presence?"

When feeling mocked or rejected for my faith, Matthew 5:10 has often come to mind, "Blessed are those who are persecuted for righteousness' sake, for theirs is the kingdom of heaven." That promise can inspire prayers along the lines of, "Lord, I will endure it for Your name's sake. It is worth it to endure; in fact, it is a blessing and an honor to endure mocking and rejection for You. And I know that when I stand before You one day, it will all prove to have been worth it." How can a person know such sufferings for the Lord are worth it? Because the Word of God says so.

In times of temptation or spiritual oppression, James 4:7 might come to mind, "Submit yourselves therefore to God. Resist the devil, and he will flee from you." Notice the order James uses: effective resisting of the devil is preceded by submitting to God. Such submission may involve hightailing it out of the situation where the temptation is hitting you hard. You are not likely to overcome lust once it has gripped you if you remain logged onto the Internet in a secluded place. If alcohol is a problem for you, you may need to leave a restaurant, or at least ask for a table that does not have a view of the bar. You may ask, how do those scenarios involve submitting to God? They do so because they are conscious decisions to get out of atmospheres where you are prone to fall into sin. You exit such places for the Lord, and in doing so, you submit to the Lord. You will also likely find yourself praying through such a scenario. For example, "Lord, this is not a good place for me to be right now. Strengthen my steps as I move away from here. I don't want anything to do with what the devil is trying to draw me into right now. I resist him. Guide my steps, Lord."

Other examples of using scripture in prayer are:
- Genesis 1:1, for when I am feeling hopeless. Is anything too hard for the One who

created the heavens and the earth (an idiom that means "everything")?

- Matthew 6:33, for when I am worried about paying the bills.
- The book of Habakkuk, for when the TV news makes it seem like the world is spinning out of control.

Another good example from my wife Nancy's prayer life is Psalm 91:4. She often prays that God will cover people with His feathers.

Praying Scripture lets us know we are praying in accordance with the mind of God. After all, prayer to the living God is prayer to the One who ultimately wrote the Scriptures. When the Christians in Acts 4 referenced Psalm 2 in their prayer, they did so in such terms, acknowledging that when David spoke the words they were citing, he spoke them by the Holy Spirit. These brothers and sisters in Christ interpreted their circumstances on the basis of what the Word says. Their example teaches us that life is properly viewed through the lens of Scripture.

How Scripture Explained Their Circumstances

Psalm 2:1-2 speaks of political plotting in opposition to the Lord's Anointed One. Some of the people praying in Acts 4 had been with Jesus during His life on earth. Jesus was the Christ—the Anointed One—and these disciples had seen the sort of opposition prophesied in Psalm 2 happen to their Lord. They may have been tempted to think their world of the past three years had suddenly spun out of control, but the Scriptures informed them otherwise. David, 1,000 years before the birth of Jesus, had spoken of things these disciples had seen unfold before their very eyes through Herod, Pontius Pilate, the Gentiles, and the Jews. The Scriptures informed these followers' understanding of the world around them, both in the things that happened to *Jesus* and in the things that were presently happening to *them.*

Not only did these prayer warriors allow the Scriptures to reveal an understanding of their surroundings, but they also prayed in light of the knowledge the Scriptures gave them. A scripturally uninformed prayer might have found a roomful of people praying that God would make all these fearful things go away. But the Scriptures told these believers that the difficult things they were seeing were *supposed* to happen, that God's hand and plan had predestined them (v. 28). That understanding informed the way they prayed, which was not for safety or deliverance but for boldness to speak God's Word in the midst of the difficulty. They prayed, "And now, Lord, look upon their threats and grant to your servants to continue to speak your word with all boldness, while you stretch out your hand to heal, and signs and wonders are performed through the name of your holy servant Jesus" (vv. 29-30).

These believers had what we would call today a biblical worldview. They understood that God is the Creator of this world, has a plan for it, and is working that plan. They grasped that man has created a breach in his relationship with God by sinning, that Jesus came to heal that breach by paying for our sins, and that message must get out. They were confident the Bible is true and tells us everything we need to know to understand human nature and world events and God.

Conclusion

As a Christian, you may believe the Bible is true, but do you evaluate life on the basis of what Scripture says? You may view it as important for "religion," but when it comes to explaining 21ˢᵗ century life, the Bible may seem to you to be somewhat antiquated. Or you may see it as a book of wisdom but not the final authority in matters of life and faith. Such a failure to give the Bible its due trust and respect leads to embracing things like astrology and psychic hotlines for direction, and pre-marital sex, easy divorces, and other non-biblical things. The Bible is *God's* Word; it is true, inerrant and infallible. The Word of God *judges* everything, right down to the thoughts and intents of our hearts. It is the only authoritative source of wisdom and when we treat it as such, we will know how to pray properly.

We are engaged in a spiritual battle. As we fight that battle on our knees, it is essential that we trust God's Word, submit to its authority, and pray in light of what it says. May doing so be a well-used weapon in your arsenal.

THOUGHTS & PRAYERS

_____

_____

_____

_____

_____

_____

_____

_____

_____

_____

_____

_____

_____

_____

_____

_____

_____

_____

_____

THOUGHTS & PRAYERS

_____

_____

_____

_____

_____

_____

_____

_____

_____

_____

_____

_____

_____

_____

_____

_____

_____

_____

_____

_____

CHAPTER 3

PRAYING IN LIGHT OF GOD'S BIG PLAN

How do you view God's involvement in your life? Do you think of it in terms of how He *treats* you? How He *provides* for you? How He *guides* you? How He *blesses* you? Is your view of God's involvement in your life all about *your* life?

I must admit, I have often pursued God with such a view. Oftentimes my prayers have been largely about things like what my life's work would be, where I should go to college or seminary, whom I would marry, whether I even *would* marry, whether I would have a pleasant suburban family existence, how much I would like God to bless me, etc.

On one hand, such a view of things may be natural and unavoidable. After all, we process life with a brain that resides in this body, with five senses through which we experience the world. We are very aware of how things affect us personally. And there certainly are many biblical examples of people praising God for good things He has done in their lives. Scripture does talk about God giving us the desires of our hearts when we delight in Him. He promises blessings on His people, and blessings are things we experience personally. But on the other hand, there is more to it than just that.

In this chapter, we are going to consider that our lives are about more than ourselves. Yes, God saves us as individuals. He loves us deeply and intimately and personally; He has a plan for our individual lives. But all of that fits within something much bigger than any of us. These early Christians in Acts 4:23-31 were certainly experiencing spiritual warfare personally, even as we do today. The arrest and threats that prompted this prayer presented them with a frightening situation in their immediate context, a situation that could have meant suffering for any of them at any time. But they knew their difficulty involved something bigger than themselves. It was bigger than God's provision for just *them*, bigger than His protection of *them*, bigger than His plan for *them*.

If these believers had understood things only in terms of their own personal lives, they might have missed the importance of what they were experiencing and may have backed out of the difficulty, griping and complaining at God for allowing them to go through such adversity. They did none of that. Rather, they saw their own experience within the big plan of God.

What is that big plan of God? It is that people would come to know how to be reconciled to Him through faith in Jesus Christ and become His disciples. Between Jesus' commission for His disciples to "go into all the world and make disciples of all nations" (Matthew 28:19) and His promise of the Holy Spirit to empower His people to be His witnesses (Acts 1:8), it is clear that Jesus wants believers to do more than seek their own personal blessings. He wants us to shine His light into a dark world. These early Christians prayed in light of God's big plan, and that is the third smooth stone in the arsenal of the prayer warrior. Notice their request in verse 29.

And now, Lord, look upon their threats and grant to your servants to continue to speak your word with all boldness.

What was the word they sought to continue speaking with all boldness? Consider that Peter and John had been arrested for ministering and preaching in the name of Jesus. They told of how the prophets had spoken of Him and that salvation was found in Him. The word these praying saints wanted to continue speaking was the glory of Jesus and the good news of salvation through Him. They wanted the world to know of Jesus. This was prayer in light of God's big plan.

Since God is working this big plan, we need to grasp a few things as we pray and live our lives. First, it is important to understand that God is in control, even when our circumstances are difficult—when it seems things are spinning out of control. These early Christians recognized that Herod, Pontius Pilate, the Gentiles, and the Jews had all come against Jesus *by the hand and predetermined plan of God* (v. 28). Clearly, these saints saw their own struggles in that same light. The predetermined opposition to Jesus was continuing upon His followers. Nevertheless, they grasped that the severity of their difficulties was trumped by the importance of God's big plan, and they prayed accordingly.

Now, the fact that God is in control may lead us to believe that whatever we go through will eventually make sense to us—and we will one day look back and say, "*Now* I understand." While 1 Corinthians 13:9-12 leads me to believe that will eventually be the case, there is no guarantee it will happen in this life. A good example is provided by the Old Testament character, Job.

Job had everything but his life taken away from him. Through nearly the entire book that bears his name, he simply wants to know why such awful things have come upon him. Meanwhile, his wife tells him he should just curse God and die, and his three friends provide chapter after chapter of seemingly endless (and often heartless) speculations on the reason for Job's condition. Job never does get an answer to why he is enduring such suffering. Ultimately, he comes to a place where he repents of having been so brash as to ask God why. God does end up giving him a double portion of all he had lost, yet Job never does get an answer to the question, *Why?*

Throughout history, believers have been persecuted for their faith. That still happens in our modern world. Some such persecution has been, and is, unto death. When those who face such oppression draw their last breath, they do so without being given a panoramic view of how their suffering fits into God's plan. They die in faith.

In the first church I pastored, there was an elderly woman who was generally joyful. She loved coming to church and was known as the "Candy Lady," for she always gave pieces of candy to the children. I had many pleasant conversations with her; sometimes about the meaning of something I had said in my sermon that morning, other times about what was going on in her life. Behind her smile was the pain of a son having been murdered years earlier. She never learned who did it or why. To this day, I long to find those answers for her but I never have and neither had she before going to be with the Lord.

The reality is that we may have difficult life experiences where we will *never* know in *this* life what God's purpose was. For now, we trust that all things work together for good, for those who love God and are called according to His purpose (Romans 8:28). We walk by faith, not sight (2 Corinthians 5:7).

A second thing we need to grasp as we pray and live our lives is that those who oppress God's people only play into His hand. The opponents of Jesus mentioned in v. 27 had thought *they* were in charge and in control of the situation as they opposed the Lord. In reality, they had only done what God had planned to take place (v. 28). Just think of the amazing things that resulted from their actions, things they certainly never intended to happen.

- The Son of God accomplished His mission: He died for our sins.
- Jesus then arose, conquering sin and death and proving who He was.
- The Lord ascended back to the Father, and those who thought they were in control will one day stand before Him.
- The Holy Spirit came to indwell and fill believers so that we can be Jesus' witnesses, keeping going that which the men who thought *they* were in charge had tried to stop.

It was a total fail for those who opposed Jesus, and God's plan marched on. They played right into God's hands. That happens today too when believers are made to suffer for their faith. God never thinks, "Oh, no! They've really got me now! My plan has been stopped in its tracks!" No, His will for our lives and how we fit into His big plan is *never* stopped, no matter what we may face.

Even if you should be put to death for your faith, your oppressors—unless they repent—will one day see you in the presence of the Lord in glory and will beg for a drop of water they will never get. And on top of that, your persecution will inspire others to serve more faithfully, leading others into a knowledge of Jesus and seeing the church that people had tried to snuff out continue to grow. Yes, God is in control and those who oppress His people only play into His hand.

There is a third thing we need to grasp as we pray and live our lives, and it is this: For the faithful believer, no difficulty is ever wasted. I love how these early believers had a grasp on that truth. In the account of their prayer, we find them *knowing* that God is working His plan and that their lives are directly involved in it. Hence, the threats against them simply will not stop them. They are not confused by their suffering. They are, rather, confident about their participation in God's big plan.

Sometimes, when things do not turn out as we had either imagined or wanted, we might find ourselves asking, "What was *that* all about?" That can be a shortsighted, me-focused question, for God is never wasteful with the circumstances He brings or allows into our lives.

My first pastoral position was everything I hoped for in a pastorate. The church grew numerically and spiritually. People came to faith in Christ. People got involved in serving the Lord in various ways, from vacation Bible schools to a short-term mission trip to Mexico. But in the middle of all of that, the Lord seemed to call me to return to the area where my wife and I met at seminary and start a church. I was both nervous about taking the risk of leaving a thriving ministry and excited to see what God might do in a new church. What ensued was ten years that never saw growth beyond a young start-up and, ultimately, the shutting down of that church. I asked the Lord numerous times, "What was THAT all about?" The results were certainly not what *I* wanted, nor what *I* thought *would* or *should* have happened. I was expecting the Spirit of God to do a work in our midst that would prompt people to ask me, "How did you do this?" and I would answer, "I cannot explain that. *God* did this." A church that floundered and fizzled was not part of the deal, so to speak.

But then I think of Acts 8, where God pulled a man named Philip away from a revival in Samaria to go share Christ with one man on a desert road. The fact is, in our church plant, small and temporary as it had been, several people did come to faith in Christ, two of whom have since gone home to be with the Lord. While I was being selfishly disappointed, God was saving people for eternity. The difficulties we go through are not for nothing. They are never wasted by God.

Of course, if you go entirely *against* the will of God—if you foolishly blow all your money with unwise spending or if you live a sexually immoral life and get an STD or destroy your marriage—none of that will thwart God's big plan, but no one can promise you that those self-imposed difficulties will not be a waste of your life.

The life of Samson demonstrates what I mean (Judges 13-16). He lived a fleshly life that found him tied to two pillars in a Philistine temple, his eyes having been gouged out by his captors who had tremendous fun mocking their now-blind-and-bound former tormentor. God would still use Samson to bring down the Philistine temple upon the enemies of God's people, but Samson would be crushed to death along with them. Samson might have had a more joyous victory and much better ending to his life had he taken his role as God's man more seriously. But if you walk with God and suffer for it, Scripture allows me to say that such suffering will never be wasted, even if you do not understand its purpose this side of heaven.

Conclusion

As you fight the spiritual battle, you may face the temptation to think that you are nothing—that God could never use you, that you are an unforgivable failure. Disappointments and unanswered questions may leave you filled with doubt and fear and discouragement. Let me say to you (and to myself), reject all of that. Pray in light of God's big plan for this world, a plan in which you, as a believer in Jesus Christ, are directly involved and have a God-ordained role to play, even when you cannot see it.

THOUGHTS & PRAYERS

THOUGHTS & PRAYERS

_____

_____

_____

_____

_____

_____

_____

_____

_____

_____

_____

_____

_____

_____

_____

_____

_____

_____

_____

CHAPTER 4

PRAYING IN LIGHT OF GOD'S MISSION FOR YOU

We have just looked at verse 29. As we continue to examine this text, imagine that you do not know how the verse ends. It *begins* like this:

And now, Lord, look upon their threats and grant...

Grant what? If you had never read this verse, what might you think the people praying that prayer would be asking of the Lord, given their tough circumstances? Might the prayer have continued, "grant us safety from those who are threatening us"? That might seem to be a reasonable request. How about "grant us revenge for the arrests and the psychological damage of their threats against us?" Might such requests have gotten a few *amens*?

No doubt, some people might pray such things in a tense and potentially dangerous situation. Would you? Would I? These early Christians did not. They had a much different idea in mind than some of us might have had. We can see it in the last part of verse 29:

...grant to your servants to continue to speak your word with all boldness...

These brothers and sisters in Christ did not seem concerned about their own safety at all. If they were, that concern was not strong enough to warrant mention as they were pouring out their hearts to God regarding their difficult predicament.

Their prayer was bold, showing they had an undaunted commitment to the Lord. They were not praying this for other people, for the church as a whole, or for some unnamed missionaries preaching the gospel "out there." They themselves were the servants of God referenced in verse 29. These individual servants who made up the organization of that local church desired to speak God's Word with all boldness—to persevere faithfully in the very thing that might have gotten them into life-threatening trouble with the authorities. They were praying in light of God's mission for themselves. That is the fourth smooth stone for prayer warriors—praying in light of God's mission for you.

We saw in the previous chapter how this early church knew that God's big plan was for His people to be a witness to the world for Jesus. The Lord made this clear just prior to His ascension. Now, the treatment of Peter and John by the authorities demonstrated that this would be a dangerous mission. Telling others about Jesus might get one grabbed off the street and thrown into prison, an intimidating prospect for sure. It would require boldness from God if the mission were to be carried out. And how else might the mission be carried out except by the faithfulness of the individuals who make up the church. While praying in light of God's big picture plan, these believers prayed for boldness for the servants who would carry out that plan. They themselves were those very servants. This was a prayer in light of their own individual involvements in God's worldwide mission. One way for us to suffer spiritual defeat is to allow ourselves to wind up on the sidelines where things seem safe. The *world* would love that, for it would mean they would not have to listen to the gospel they find so offensive. Our *flesh* would love it, for all manner of persecution for our faith would disappear. The *devil* would love it, for our effectiveness for the glory of God would be neutralized. So it is imperative for our spiritual vitality that we remain active in God's will for our lives. This requires prayer. We can learn some things from these early believers about that.

One thing we can learn is that praying in light of God's mission for our individual lives begins with knowing our place before God. Notice how the Christians in Acts 4 described themselves to God in verse 29, "grant to your *servants.*" The word that the ESV translates "servants" is the Greek word *doulos*, which means *slave*. They knew God was their Master and they were subservient to Him. Therefore, they submitted to His will for their lives.

The Bible uses several varieties of human relationship to describe the one we have with God. For example, God is *Abba*, an intimate Greek word for "Father," and we are His children if we are in Christ. Believers are friends, even brothers, of Jesus. God is our refuge, our helper, our provider, and our Savior. All those things are true; they are biblical. But they are not the whole picture. When we treat them like they *are* the whole picture, we wind up with a skewed view of God and where we stand before Him.

The world certainly has a skewed view of God. They either perceive Him as a cruel tyrant, or they misconstrue Him toward being a tolerant, manageable love *meister*. Perhaps you have heard people distinguish between the "Old Testament God," whom they view as a tyrant, and Jesus, whom they view as being all about love and tolerance. Such a distorted view of Jesus betrays an ignorance of the full scope of what the Bible teaches us about Him. Sadly, it seems to be a common view among even Christians these days.

God is holy, righteous, and just. Sinners that we are, we deserve only judgment from Him, yet He shows us mercy. Every breath we take is undeserved and only happens because of God's mercy toward us. God is not some giant, sappy smiley face. He is our Master. Whatever else is true of God, we have an incomplete view of Him if we forget that He is our Lord, and we are His servants. Even a cursory reading of the Bible shows this to be true.

God is our Master is a truth from which we draw two implications. First, as servants, our lot in life is to do our Master's will. That is what this Acts 4 church was seeking to do. Jesus had made the will of God clear when He said, "You will be my witnesses" (Acts 1:8). The prayer of these first century Jerusalem saints portrayed an understanding of the magnitude of that calling. We can see it in their concern, not that the authorities might make good on their threats, but that they themselves might lose heart and falter on the Master's mission. They prayed for boldness that was beyond themselves but which they knew God could supply in abundance. They prayed in light of God's mission for them.

The D-Day invasion of Normandy in World War II required some troops to storm beachheads under heavy fire from cliffs above, with virtually no cover to protect them. Steven Spielberg seems to have captured the experience in his film *Saving Private Ryan*, which portrays a barrage of bullets felling Allied forces in their amphibious landing craft, while wading ashore, and all along the beach. There was nowhere to hide. It is horrifying to watch, knowing that the film portrays what actually happened to living, breathing souls who all had families and loved ones, and far different hopes and dreams than what they faced that day. Why would those men brave such a thing? Perhaps there were some who were altruistic, willing to face a high-percentage chance of death for the sake of the mission. But for those whose fear would have overridden such altruism, there was the fact that their commander ordered them to do it. General Eisenhower oversaw this plan, and the soldiers were under his authority. As it turned out, everyone who went ashore that day, whether they lived or died, helped accomplish something essential. That battle became a turning point in the war.

God has infinitely more authority over us than Eisenhower had over those men under his command. Ike may have been the supreme commander of the Allied forces, but God rules the universe. He is our King, and we are His subjects; He is the Potter, and we are the clay. He is our Master; we are His servants—the servant's lot in life is to do the will of his master.

The second implication is that God has a mission for each of us to carry out. Our individual missions are part of God's big redemptive plan for mankind in which we are to be witnesses for Jesus. Within that big plan, God has designed for you a part to play. We can see that in Ephesians 2:10:

For we are his workmanship, created in Christ Jesus for good works, which God prepared beforehand, that we should walk in them.

In other words, the Master Craftsman had a purpose in mind for you before you even came to be.

My wife loves to play the flute when we worship at church. Somewhere back in time, a craftsman made her flute with a specific purpose in mind. Now, people may come along and use that flute for other purposes. Perhaps someone would want to use it as a mini flagpole while marching in a parade. Someone else might think it would make a good corkball bat in a pinch. Another person might view it as a fine replacement for a broken leg on an end table. However, that flute is at its best when used for what it was originally designed. When it is skillfully played to make music, it fulfills its intended mission and is a blessing to all who hear it.

God is your Craftsman, and when you came to faith in Jesus, you became a new creation with a purpose He intended for you. God fashioned you anew with good works in mind for you to do. The world would have you do things other than what the Craftsman made you to do, things that would please *them*. Your flesh would have you do things other than what the Craftsman intended, things that would please *you*. The devil would have you do things other than what the Craftsman purposed, things that would rob the Craftsman of His glory and steal from you the joy of being what He made you to be. You will be at your best only when you do what the Craftsman designed you to do, even when doing so may potentially put you in harm's way.

God's creation of you as a new creature involves both serving the church and sharing the gospel. For serving the church He gave you spiritual gifts. Those gifts are to be used for building up His body, the church. As you seek to serve the Lord and His church, you may discover that some things you do might not go so well, while other things you do may bless and edify God's people. The latter will be an indication of how the Craftsman has gifted you for service in His body.

Countless books have been written on the subject of spiritual gifts. This is not one of them. Our purpose is to examine a particular prayer in Scripture, one that some devoted followers of Christ prayed during a time of great difficulty. We are seeking to learn from them and their prayer. But since one thing we have learned is that they prayed in light of God's mission for them, knowing how God has gifted you comes into play with that. Therefore, please allow me to direct you to two passages of Scripture for further study on the matter of spiritual gifts in the body of Christ: Romans 12:4-8 and 1 Corinthians 12:4-11.

Along with serving the church, God's plan for you as a new creation is to be a witness for Jesus to the world. As He leads you into situations and encounters with people, always be prepared "to make a defense to anyone who asks you for a reason for the hope that is in you; yet do it with gentleness and respect" (1 Peter 3:15). Whether He opens doors of opportunity for you around the world or across the street, His purpose is that people have an opportunity to see Jesus in your life and hear the good news of salvation through Jesus from your lips. Both in serving the church and being prepared to give an answer to the world, He will lead you into your individual part within His big plan.

His plan may lead you into danger. If so, how will you assess the situation and pray about it? The Acts 4 believers clearly saw the danger in continuing to speak the Word of God to the world around them. But rather than praying for safety in that moment, they prayed for boldness to continue doing the very thing that could get them arrested or even killed.

Conclusion

If your life seems to be random, it is not. If you feel like it is meaningless, it is not. If someone has made you feel worthless, they are wrong. If you are in Christ, your life is on a mission. Are you living that way? And are you praying that way? If we would all pray in light of God's mission for us—in other words, if we were as concerned with the quality and effectiveness and endurance of our witness and service as we are with the usual kinds of things we pray for—we just might become like this early church of whom it is said, "These men turned the world upside down" (Acts 17:6).

THOUGHTS & PRAYERS

_____

_____

_____

_____

_____

_____

_____

_____

_____

_____

_____

_____

_____

_____

_____

_____

_____

_____

THOUGHTS & PRAYERS

CHAPTER 5

PRAYING IN LIGHT OF YOUR DEPENDENCE UPON GOD

Did you ever sell candy or magazines door-to-door when you were in school? If you did, you probably approached each door ready to deliver a spiel you memorized. The idea was all you had to do was recite this professionally written sales presentation and then you would fill out the order form with the customer's information and how much of your product they wanted to buy. There was no one to help you. It was all dependent upon you simply saying the right words and, of course, smiling. You were on your own, doing the best you could, hoping to make the sale.

If that is how we try to face the spiritual battle that seeks to hinder our service to God, we are toast! We need help, and the help we need is far greater than the professionally written sales presentation that was supposed to turn our door-to-door excursion into a cash cow. We need God Himself to show up in power. Nothing short will fend off the attacks from principalities and powers that our flesh is incapable of fighting. Hence, when we pray, may it be in light of our dependence upon God. This is the prayer warrior's fifth smooth stone.

As we have noted numerous times in this study, the praying Christians shown in Acts chapter 4 faced serious opposition in their efforts to live for Jesus. The battle was intense; their very lives were being threatened. But they knew their mission was to be witnesses for the Lord, so they pressed on, praying for boldness (as we saw in the last chapter). Now, in verse 30 we find them seeking the very power of God to be present in their endeavors. They knew they needed that. We need it, too.

In *their* case, they prayed specifically for signs and wonders to accompany their witness for Christ, even as they had seen happening to that point. There can be a temptation to look at a scriptural prayer request like that and try to normalize it for all people in all times and places. In other words, some may expect that God always works such visible miracles through His people. It is important to note that such miraculous displays are not always the way God works. In fact, looking at Scripture as a whole, signs and wonders are not the *usual* way God acts. For example, when Paul stood before Felix in Acts 24 and before Herod Agrippa in Acts 25-26, there were no signs and wonders accompanying his preaching. But that does not mean God was any less present.

Ultimately, it is not the outward manifestation of signs and wonders that we need in serving the Lord, unless God wants to work them, of course. Rather, we require the power and presence of God, whether visible manifestations are involved or not. The question for us is this: in the face of opposition from the world, the flesh, and the devil, are we trying to serve Christ simply by gritting our teeth and doing our best, or are we humbly acknowledging to God that all is lost without His involvement? Are we seeking the power of His presence? Let us take a look at just how dependent we are upon the Lord in living the Christian life.

Scriptural Evidence of Our Dependence on the Lord

The Bible presents our dependence upon the Lord for living the Christian life in both a negative and a positive sense. Consider first the negative sense. Jesus tells us what we are incapable of doing:

Abide in me, and I in you. As the branch cannot bear fruit by itself, unless it abides in the vine, neither can you, unless you abide in me. I am the vine; you are the branches. Whoever abides in me and I in him, he it is that bears much fruit, for apart from me you can do nothing. (John 15:4-5)

Jesus says, "Apart from me you can do nothing." What more evidence do we need that we are utterly dependent upon Him? Without Him we are incapable of doing anything.

Now, of course, there are things people do successfully apart from a dependence upon Christ. For instance, an atheist can build a successful business. It happens all the time. An athlete can have a stellar career without acknowledging God. An artist can revolutionize the art world while creating art that opposes the things of God. Many people who deny Christ, and even some who deny the existence of a divine being at all, are capable of doing things in this world that bring them acclaim and wealth. But notice what kinds of things Jesus was talking about. Take another look at His words from John 15, this time with words italicized for emphasis.

Abide in me, and I in you. As the branch cannot *bear fruit* by itself, unless it abides in the vine, neither can you, unless you abide in me. I am the vine; you are the branches. Whoever abides in me

and I in him, he it is that *bears much fruit*, for apart
from me you can do nothing.

Jesus was talking specifically about bearing spiritual
fruit. His point was that no one can do the things of
God—such as good works of eternal value and triumph-
ing in spiritual warfare—apart from Him. Hence, we
cannot worship God apart from Christ. We are incapable of producing any spiritually worthwhile or valuable
thing in ourselves. We cannot serve or please or know
God apart from Christ. We humans are prone to making lists of dos and don'ts to quantify what qualifies as
spiritual success. But our success in walking with the
Lord is not about following a list of rules; it is not about
religious rites, rituals, or appearances. It is about people
with no capacity for bearing fruit for God being *given*
that capacity by Christ, and it comes—not from paying
lip service to Him or being associated with the right
people and jumping through all the right hoops—but
from abiding in Him and He in us. It comes from a life
of relationship, of fellowship with Him; a life that is lived
for Him, communes with Him, and draws from Him.
Jesus is to us what the vine is to the branch, the source of
life and fruit-bearing ability.

The church in Acts 4 was led by—and partially con-
sisted of—people who had walked with Jesus, God in the
flesh. And now they were praying to God, not as a distant
deity or religious ideal, but as One going out witnessing
with them. That is abiding. And so, they prayed for boldness (v. 29), but not just for an infusion to be taken out and
used the way a car fills up with gas and drives away from
the pump that filled it. They knew they needed Him to
go *with* them. They needed His *presence* and power at work
in their ministry of the gospel.

Verse 30 bears this out, giving the context in which the boldness they sought was to thrive:

> *...while you stretch out your hand to heal, and signs and wonders are performed through the name of your holy servant Jesus.*

They were keenly aware of their absolute dependence upon His hand to work on their behalf as they lived out their calling in the face of spiritual opposition.

Our battle is no less severe. We are every bit as dependent as they were for we too can do nothing apart from Christ. That is the negative sense in which the Bible presents our dependence upon the Lord. What about the positive sense? We find an expression of it in Philippians 4:10-13:

> *I rejoiced in the Lord greatly that now at length you have revived your concern for me. You were indeed concerned for me, but you had no opportunity. Not that I am speaking of being in need, for I have learned in whatever situation I am to be content. I know how to be brought low, and I know how to abound. In any and every circumstance, I have learned the secret of facing plenty and hunger, abundance and need. I can do all things through him who strengthens me.*

Whereas Christ said we can do *nothing* apart from Him, Paul states he can do *all* things through Christ. Once again, we need to take note of exactly what is being talked about in this passage for it is often misused.

Paul is thanking the Philippians for supporting his ministry financially, but as much as he appreciates them, he acknowledges it is the *Lord* who sustains him, not money. He is saying, "I've learned to endure whatever it takes to fulfill the Lord's mission for my life. I can be rich or poor, hungry or full, imprisoned or free, because I can do all things through Him who strengthens me."

This promise of being able to do all things through Christ is often applied over just about any walk of life. I once heard of a pole vaulter on a high school track and field team who had this verse emblazoned on his vaulting pole. However, Paul's words are not an assurance that we can succeed through Christ at anything we attempt in life. His statement is much more focused than that—we can do whatever is required of us to fulfill our calling through the strength Christ gives us.

To sum up these negative and positive senses in which God's Word portrays our dependence upon the Lord, we cannot bear fruit for Christ apart from abiding in Him, and whatever He calls us to do we can accomplish through His strength.

The prideful heart of man wants to end Philippians 4:13 after the first five words: "I can do all things." Or "There is nothing I can't do if I put my mind to it." "If I just believe in myself, then anything is possible." The world may tell us, "If you dream it, you can do it," but that is simply not true. We cannot be anything we want to be. We are neither so talented nor so versatile. We may have the freedom to *try* to be whatever we want to be, but the harsh reality is that each of us has limitations—even great and vast limitations. This may sound like a wet blanket statement, but it is true.

Consider this example from my love for basketball. If I decided I wanted to be an NBA player, I could believe in myself and put my mind to accomplishing that until the cows come home. I can certainly dream it, but can I do it? I am here to tell you that no matter how much I believe in myself, it is not happening. Now, if I had wanted that badly enough when I was younger, I certainly could have worked very hard and tried to succeed at it. But the odds are that I would have failed. I could have dreamt about it all night every night and daydreamed about it all day every day, but that would not have made me an NBA player.

If that sounds like a wet blanket to you, allow me to remove that blanket and dry it out. You and I are called to something infinitely greater than playing professional sports (or being a movie star, rock star, President, or any number of great things people dream about becoming). We are called to lives that can make an eternal impact as we represent Jesus in this world. How does Paul's "I can do all things" statement apply to that? It applies like this: You can be whatever the Lord calls you to be and do whatever He wants you to do, and you can stand up under any oppression that may come to you as a result of pursuing your call, and you can endure whatever circumstances you may be required to endure because the One who *calls* you is *with* you and will *strengthen* you. Without Him, you can do nothing. With Him, you can do *all* things.

Moses understood these truths long before Jesus came to earth or Paul was an apostle. In Exodus 33:1-3, God tells Moses to press on with the children of Israel on their way from Egypt to the promised land, "a land flowing with milk and honey," which God had promised to Abraham, Isaac, Jacob, and their descendants. God also promised He would send an angel ahead of them to drive out the land's current inhabitants. It seemed nothing would stand in the way of Israel possessing the land God had promised them. No doubt, these words from God were things Moses wanted to hear and in which he could find comfort and assurance. Perhaps he was raring to get on with it. But then, God dropped a bombshell: "I will not go up among you, lest I consume you on the way, for you are a stiff-necked people." That changed everything. What had happened?

Just prior to God's words in Exodus 33, the children of Israel had grown weary in waiting for Moses to return from the mountain top where he had gone to meet with God. In their impatience, they built the golden calf and worshiped it. God would keep His promise of delivering them into the promised land, for He is faithful even when we are not (cf. 2 Timothy 2:13). But He would not accompany the people to the land. This is where Moses displayed an understanding of the principles that centuries later would be recorded in John 15 and Philippians 4. He said to the Lord,

> *"If your presence will not go with me, do not bring us up from here. For how shall it be known that I have found favor in your sight, I and your people? Is it not in your going with us, so that we are distinct, I and your people, from every other people on the face of the earth?"* (Exodus 33:15-16)

Moses knew that the calling of Israel was to live in the land as a nation that would be distinguished from all other nations by belonging to God. How could they live out their calling without the Lord's presence among them? To go on their own, even if God were to assure their safe arrival and successful entry, would make them just another nation. They could only be what God intended them to be by the power and presence of God. If God would not go with them, neither would Moses go. What would be the point?

Similarly, the church in Acts 4 was saying, in effect, "We can speak the words, but we cannot really be Your witnesses if You are not involved. We *need* You, Lord. We need Your *power*. We need Your *presence*. We are helpless without You." And they were absolutely right.

Conclusion

The spiritual battles we face are intended to derail the work of God through us in this world. We cannot win spiritual battles with fleshly strength or human ingenuity. We need the *presence* of God in what we are doing. We must have the *power* of God in our endeavors. If we would be wise, whenever we cry out to God in prayer in the midst of our battles, we would have in our arsenal—and would make frequent use of—the practice of praying in light of our full dependence upon God. Not to do so is to rush into the battle proudly thinking we can win on our own. And as Proverbs 16:18 warns us, "Pride goes before destruction, and a haughty spirit before a fall." Our dependence upon God is one of the most basic truths in all of existence.

THOUGHTS & PRAYERS

_____

_____

_____

_____

_____

_____

_____

_____

_____

_____

_____

_____

_____

_____

_____

_____

_____

_____

_____

_____

THOUGHTS & PRAYERS

_____

_____

_____

_____

_____

_____

_____

_____

_____

_____

_____

_____

_____

_____

_____

_____

_____

_____

EPILOGUE

THEY PRAYED
AND GOD ANSWERED

In this book we have looked at a first century gathering of Christians who were enmeshed in the spiritual battle which sought to hinder and derail their effectiveness for the gospel and the glory of Christ. Their battle was seen in the form of intense pressure from people in authority who were seeking to stomp out all preaching done in the name of Jesus. The response of these believers was not to stop preaching but to gather with one another and take their situation to God in prayer. Our examination of that event has revealed five biblical understandings these believers had come to realize as they brought their request to God. We have likened these to the five smooth stones that David carried into battle against Goliath 1,000 years earlier. To recap, the *five smooth stones* are:

1. Praying in light of who God is
2. Praying in light of what God's Word says
3. Praying in light of God's big plan
4. Praying in light of God's mission for you
5. Praying in light of your dependence upon God

As they prayed for boldness to speak God's Word and for God to be present with them in power, God answered.

And when they had prayed, the place in which they were gathered together was shaken, and they were all filled with the Holy Spirit and continued to speak the word of God with boldness. (Acts 4:31)

God's answer was to fill them with the Holy Spirit, giving them boldness to obey God rather than man. That is God's provision for the battle—then and now.

The Power of the Holy Spirit's Filling

When God is present in power, it will be in the fullness of His Holy Spirit. We get a glimpse of that in what Jesus said right before He ascended back to heaven: "You will receive power when the Holy Spirit has come upon you, and you will be my witnesses in Jerusalem and in all Judea and Samaria, and to the end of the earth" (Acts 1:8).

How would a small band of nobodies be the Lord's witnesses to a world that would largely oppose their message? They would do it by the power they receive when the Holy Spirit has come upon them. How could a group of about one hundred twenty people (Acts 1:15) in Jerusalem be His witnesses, not only in Jerusalem, which would be a big job itself, but extending outward through the regions of Judea and Samaria and the ends of the earth? How could such an undertaking be possible before there were any ways to communicate long distance with masses of people? The passage does not lay out any logistics. Those would unfold as believers walked by faith going forward. But the power for accomplishing this task would come from the fullness of the Holy Spirit.

This Was Not a New Idea

This idea of the Holy Spirit coming upon people with power to do God's work in this world did not originate on that day when Jesus made the promise to His disciples just prior to ascending through the clouds. God had been empowering people for service by His Holy Spirit for generations leading up to that time. For instance, in the book of Judges, which covers events hundreds of years before the birth of Christ, we read of the Spirit of the Lord being upon Othniel as he judged Israel (3:10). Again, in Judges we are told that the Spirit of the Lord "clothed Gideon" as God prepared him to deliver Israel from the Midianites (6:34). The book moves on to tell us of Samson, "the Spirit of the Lord began to stir him" prior to his becoming a judge in Israel (13:25). The account then goes on to tell of Samson's years as a judge and mentions three times (14:6, 19; 15:14) that "the Spirit of the Lord rushed upon him" to enable him to do great feats of strength.

It is not only in the book of Judges that we read of such things. When Samuel anointed David with oil as the next king of Israel, 1 Samuel 16:13 says that "the Spirit of the LORD rushed upon David from that day forward." In the New Testament, the angel Gabriel told Mary that she, though a virgin, would give birth to the Son of the Most High because "the Holy Spirit will come upon you, and the power of the Most High will overshadow you" (Luke 1:35).

All of these and others were able to do what God called them to do because the Holy Spirit came upon them. We cannot truly do the works of God in the power of the flesh; we need God's Spirit. As Zechariah 4:6 says, "Not by might, nor by power, but by my Spirit, says the LORD of hosts."

The Filling of the Holy Spirit

This early church in Acts 4 found themselves in a situation where fulfilling the call to be witnesses for Jesus meant that they would face threats from the authorities. It would be easy for a person in such circumstances to say,

"Well, being a witness for Jesus here is more dangerous than it might be someplace else, so we would be justified in living out our faith incognito." We have seen how they did not take that approach. Rather, they asked God for boldness to keep on preaching in the name of Jesus. God's answer to their prayer was not merely to give them a steely resolve and a dose of inner courage; He filled them with His Spirit.

Now, as vital as this matter of the filling of the Holy Spirit is, it has sadly become a point of division in the body of Christ. Here is a very simplified explanation of the three main understandings of how the power of the Holy Spirit works in the life of the believer. These descriptions are what I have gathered over the years through study and fellowship with believers in the various camps.

- PENTECOSTALS hold that a believer is baptized with the Holy Spirit separately from, and sometime after the point of, salvation. This is often referred to as a "second blessing." They view speaking in tongues as a necessary sign that a person has received the Holy Spirit and tend to expect manifestations of what are often called the "sign gifts" (tongues, prophecy, healings, etc.) in their worship services.

- CHARISMATICS do not generally seek a second blessing in regard to the baptism with the Holy Spirit, nor do they tend to view tongues as a necessary sign of such baptism. They do embrace the 'sign gifts' as normative for the church today.

- NON-CHARISMATICS, who could also be called non-Pentecostals, believe a person is baptized with the Holy Spirit at the moment of salvation. There is typically no expectation of any supernatural phenomena to accompany that experience. A common expression among this group is "one baptism, many fillings," with the "fillings" of the Spirit often being understood to mean not that a person gets anything more of the Spirit than he already has, but that the Spirit gets more of the *person* as he/she yields to the control of the Holy Spirit. Non-charismatics often believe the "sign gifts" ended when the apostles had all died and the Scriptures had been received from the Lord.

To reiterate, this is a very simplified explanation. These are thumbnail sketches of the tendencies of each group. Certainly, there are people within each camp who would say these descriptions do not entirely describe their position. And, of course, there would be people whose views would incorporate details from more than one of these groups. We may sometimes tend to draw the lines of demarcation between our differences on these issues with too thick of a pen. Perhaps we do that on other issues as well.

All things considered, the issue, as I see it, breaks down into two basic questions:

1. When does a person receive the Holy Spirit?
2. What (if anything) does that experience look like?

We will look at a few Scriptures that shine some light on the matter.

Those who are in the flesh cannot please God. You, however, are not in the flesh but in the Spirit, if in fact the Spirit of God dwells in you. **Anyone who does not have the Spirit of Christ does not belong to him.** *(Romans 8:8-9, bold text added for emphasis)*

It is clear from this text that anyone who does not have the Holy Spirit is not saved. Therefore, a person *must* receive the Holy Spirit in some sense at the moment of salvation. But, as clear as that is, it is not the entire story, for the New Testament speaks of three different ways that we have the Holy Spirit. I was introduced to this concept several years ago through R. A. Torrey's book, *The Baptism with the Holy Spirit.*

"If you love me, you will keep my commandments. And I will ask the Father, and he will give you another Helper, to be with you forever, even the Spirit of truth, whom the world cannot receive, because it neither sees him nor knows him. You know him, for he dwells **with** *you and will be* **in** *you." (John 14:15-17, bold text added for emphasis)*

Here we see two of the three ways in which we have the Holy Spirit. Jesus says, "He dwells **with** you and will be **in** you." The Holy Spirit was **with** the apostles in the person of Jesus, but the day was coming soon when Jesus would ascend back to heaven, and the Holy Spirit would come **in** to them. For some of His disciples, this seems to have happened between the time of His resurrection and ascension when He suddenly appeared among them in a locked room, breathed on them and said, "Receive the Holy Spirit" (John 20:19-22). The fact that those words were linked to His having breathed on them strongly suggests that their receiving of the Holy Spirit happened then and there. Why else would He have breathed on them?

That event took place during a special, brief period of time in earth's history: forty days between Jesus' resurrection from the dead and His ascension back to the Father. There has been no other time on earth like those few weeks, and we can expect that unique things might have taken place during that time. For the rest of us, though, Paul's words in Romans 8:8-9—written a fair amount of time after Jesus physically left this earth—describe the age in which we live, as we await the Lord's return. Those words tell us that anyone who is a believer has the Holy Spirit.

We could say that the Holy Spirit is **with** a person before the person is a believer. After all, it is the Spirit who draws and woos and convicts a person toward seeing the need for salvation and coming to faith in Christ (John 16:8). Once that faith is exercised, the Holy Spirit comes **in** the person, indwelling the new believer who is now a temple of the Holy Spirit (1 Corinthians 6:19). There is also a third way in which we may have the Holy Spirit.

You will receive power when the Holy Spirit has come **upon** *you, and you will be my witnesses in Jerusalem and in all Judea and Samaria, and to the end of the earth. (Acts 1:8)*

To those disciples who received the Holy Spirit in that locked room, Jesus said, "when the Holy Spirit has come **upon** you." The Holy Spirit was **in** them and would soon come **upon** them.

Putting it all together, we see that the Holy Spirit is **with** a person before he even comprehends the gospel, drawing him to a place of understanding so that he might believe. When belief occurs, the Holy Spirit then takes up residence **in** the person. Going forward from that moment, the saved person, who has the Holy Spirit within, receives power for service to the Lord and the gospel when the Holy Spirit comes **upon** him. *With, in* and *upon.*

Synonymous with what is often termed the *filling of the Holy Spirit*, it would seem that the *upon* experience is repeatable throughout the life of a believer. Paul instructs believers in Ephesians 5:18-21 to be filled with the Holy Spirit, meaning that those who already have the Spirit (per Romans 8:9) are to be filled with the Spirit continually (and the New Testament Greek calls for this to be an ongoing experience). In fact, the Acts 4 believers were present in Jerusalem on the day of Pentecost when the Holy Spirit fell upon the believers gathered there. Those people who received the Holy Spirit on Pentecost were now being filled with the Spirit as God responded to their heartfelt prayer, demonstrating that the indwelling of the Holy Spirit at salvation is not the end of the matter for the believer. The indwelt believer is to be continually filled with the Holy Spirit, and that may sometimes happen in very dramatic fashion as it did in Acts 4, though we should not attempt to formulize what the filling of the Spirit looks like. (To see how there is no formulaic experience in the filling of the Holy Spirit, note the differences between Acts 2:1-4; 4:8, 31; 9:17; 10:44-46; 13:9, 52; and 19:1-6.) Often, it looks like nothing outwardly but shows forth in effective ministry by the one so filled.

Given that Ephesians 5 commands us to be filled with the Holy Spirit, one might reasonably ask, "How do I do that?" Perhaps an entire other book could be written on that subject, but for our purposes in this book, let us consider how the people at that Acts 4 prayer meeting were filled. Their hearts were bowed to the sovereign God of the universe; they submitted to His Word in evaluating their circumstances and figuring out how to proceed faithfully in them; they desired to see God's big-picture plan for the world go forth, they desired to pursue God's place for them in that plan; and they humbly acknowledged their absolute need for the Lord's help to proceed. God responded by filling them with the Spirit.

In case you did not notice, I have just restated the five stones that are the topic of this book. They flow from lives of devotion to God—lives that want what God wants. It was into such lives of devotion, people who prioritized God's will above even their own safety, that God sent the fullness of His Spirit, and the room shook. That fullness gave them the boldness to rise from that place and carry on as representatives of Jesus in a world that often seeks to eliminate Him. If you want to be filled with the Holy Spirit so that you might do the work that God would have you do for His glory, this seems like a good place to be. And if you want to know how to pray effectively as the spiritual battle seeks to afflict you, pick up the five smooth stones and let them fly!

THOUGHTS & PRAYERS

_____

_____

_____

_____

_____

_____

_____

_____

_____

_____

_____

_____

_____

_____

_____

_____

_____

_____

_____

_____

THOUGHTS & PRAYERS

_____

_____

_____

_____

_____

_____

_____

_____

_____

_____

_____

_____

_____

_____

_____

_____

_____

_____

APPENDIX

SAMPLE PRAYERS UTILIZING THE FIVE STONES

In the Introduction to this book, we promised that the five stones can help keep a person focused on prayer when the mind might want to start wandering. I have found this to be true as I have utilized these guides in my own prayer life. What follows are three sample prayers that demonstrate how the five stones might be applied in prayers for various things. In each sample, wherever things move from one stone to another, the text is emboldened, and the number of the stone is shown in parentheses. It is not my intention that these prayers be copied or recited verbatim, but only that they help you employ the five stones in all kinds of circumstances about which you might pray.

EXAMPLE #1:
PRAYER FOR A SICK BELIEVER
(WE WILL CALL HIM NICK).

Lord, I bring my brother Nick before You in his illness. (1) **I thank You that you are the sovereign God**, the Creator of all things, and by virtue of that, Your creation is subject to You, not the other way around. That is true of illnesses too. (2) **Your Word tells us** that You accomplish all You purpose to do. My heart's desire is that You would raise up Nick quickly and that he would fully recover. But even as I ask that, I realize that You are God, and I am not. So, I make my request humbly and submit to whatever Your will may be. (3) **You have a plan for this entire planet**, Lord, that people would hear the gospel and be redeemed by faith. You know perfectly how Nick's life, and what happens in this time of illness, fits into Your plan. That knowledge is beyond me. (4) **And You have a plan for Nick's life** specifically, a plan that is part of Your bigger plan for the world. I pray that Nick would realize that plan for his life, even as he is sick in bed. There is somebody somewhere who might be impacted by Nick's faith during his time of illness. I pray You would make him strong spiritually during this time so that his life might be a beacon that shines the glory and grace of Jesus. (5) **I pray that You would strengthen and empower him** by Your Holy Spirit to shine Your light in this dark world. He needs You for that, Lord, even as I do. Thank You that You can take even an illness to get the attention of lost people so that they might become found. I pray these things in Jesus' name.

EXAMPLE #2:
PRAYER DURING A FINANCIAL STRUGGLE.

(1) **Sovereign God, Creator of all things**: You see our struggle. It is hard, Lord, but I know it is not hard for You. Money is a creation of man, and You are certainly not hindered by anything we have created. Nor are You surprised by our situation. When we got to this point, You were already here. (2) **Your Word tells us** that You know all about us. You know the number of hairs on our heads, the number of days of our lives, our thoughts before we even express them. You see every sparrow that falls to the ground, so we know You see us too. That You

would allow us to be here means that (3) **this somehow fits into Your grand plan**. Maybe someone who needs You is watching how we will handle this situation, Lord, and if we were not facing this struggle, we would never get to bear that testimony. (4) **Maybe our small part in Your plan** for this moment is to endure in trust and demonstrate how You are worthy of our faith. (5) **Help us to do it**, Lord, for we are frail and fickle and are prone to be weighed down by our problems and struggles. We cannot do this without the power of Your Holy Spirit. We ask for that power now, even as we humbly ask that You meet our need. We pray these things in Jesus' name.

EXAMPLE #3:
PRAYER FOR A STRUGGLE WITH SIN.

Lord, I come to You feeling dirty, feeling like a failure. This is Your world. (1) **You made it and are its rightful ruler**. It exists according to Your laws and principles. Likewise, my life belongs to You, and I am subject to Your Word. How I fail in that subjection again and again. I am, as the hymn says, prone to wander. You could rightfully cast me out, (2) **and yet I read in Your Word** where Jesus said He would not cast out those who are His. I know I am His; I have believed on Him as my Savior, and I rest in Your faithfulness to Your own Word, even as I am so unfaithful. Your Word assures me that when I am faithless, You abide faithful, for You cannot deny Yourself. I rest in that, but I shudder to think that I would ever test You on that or anything. I come in accordance with Your Word now, confessing my sin, believing Your promise to forgive me and cleanse me from all unrighteousness. I thank You that, (3) **in**

Your grand plan for this world, You sought me out, called me and drew me to the cross, that I might have the redemption You have provided in Your Son, even as You do for people all around me. (4) And somehow, failure that I am, **You can still use me in that plan**. I so want to be used. Please guard me from bringing reproach to Your name in the sight of others by my sin. I am a trophy of Your grace and I want to act like one. But I find that though the spirit is willing, Lord, the flesh is weak. I prove daily how I cannot bear Your fruit and live as one of Yours in my own strength. (5) **I need You so much**. Please fill me with Your Spirit and enable me to walk in victory. And when I fail again, prick my heart with a conviction that drives me back to You in confession. I pray these things in Jesus' name.

THOUGHTS & PRAYERS

_____

_____

_____

_____

_____

_____

_____

_____

_____

_____

_____

_____

_____

_____

_____

_____

_____

_____

_____

THOUGHTS & PRAYERS

NOTES

[1]Cleon L Rogers Jr. and Cleon L. Rogers III, *The New Linguistic and Exegetical Key to the Greek New Testament*, (Grand Rapids: Zondervan Publishing House), 237.

[2]"What Is Jupiter?" NASA, July 8, 2016, https://www.nasa.gov/audience/forstudents/k-4/stories/nasa-knows/what-is-jupiter-k4.html.

[3] "Solar System Sizes," NASA Science: Solar System Exploration, October 24, 2003, https://solarsystem.nasa.gov/resources/686/solar-system-sizes/.

[4] Christopher Springob, "How Does the Sun Compare to Other Stars? (Beginner)," Ask an Astronomer, Last updated February 10, 2016.

[5] Ibid.

[6] Lawrence Mykytiuk, "Archaeology Confirms 50 Real People in the Bible," BAS Library: Biblical Archaeology Society Online Archive, March/April 2014, https://www.baslibrary.org/biblical-archaeology-review/40/2/4.

[7] Ibid.

[8] Lawrence Mykytiuk, "Archaeology Confirms 3 More Bible People," BAS Library: Biblical Archaeology Society Online Archive, May/June 2017, https://www.baslibrary.org/biblical-archaeology-review/43/3/6.

Follow the author online at:

www.markdrinnenberg.com

www.facebook.com/markdrinnenbergwriter

www.instagram.com/markdrinnenbergwriter

Made in the USA
Monee, IL
11 January 2023

25084467R00056